the 365

A Personal Compass To Self Discovery & Enlightenment

Undrai Fizer, Ph.D.

foreword by Dr. Bridget Fizer

DIVINE **HOUSE**
B O O K S

ISBN: 978-0-615-85118-1

Barry and Shawn; You are my brother and sister "of another mother!" I appreciate you being a true peer of mine, in both Thought, Principle, and Mind! Love you both!

Dee & Squido; You have watched me evolve to so many dimensions of ME over the years. You have been a constant friend to my family and I, "as well as a virtual aunt" for my sons when we had no one else. Thank you for the scrapbook of all of the things I've done in my life, as well as for being a listening ear when I've complained of all of the "crazy stuff" that happened to me as well. I've never forgotten the $20 dollar bills you would leave hidden between the couch pillows for me "when my life was seemingly at a low point!" You've invested in me way before I became "Dr. Fizer!" To you, I will always be "Drai!" Love you sis! And Squido, I appreciate your quiet wisdom…

Darren; You have grown so much. I am so very proud of you. You are a living testament to what this book is truly about. I have seen you embody the essence of these pages. You have been such an inspiration to me. I love you big brother! Keep it up..

Kathy V., Jason Smith, and Chari McHenry; You all have been my partners in so many things. Craziness, Music, Ministry, Laughter, Madness, Silliness, and BECOMING. Thank you for sticking with me, quitting me, and re-joining me! Each of you have a trait of Life that I needed so much of. You all are JOYS to work with, play with, and "eat the half-price appetizers at Applebee's with!" Continue to believe in yourselves. I'm just here to be a friend to your Purposes and an encourager to your dreams. That's why y'all call me COACH! :-)

ACKNOWLEDGMENTS

Holy Spirit, I thank you for everything YOU hav accomplished within me. My efficiency, potential, and achievements, are of no surprise to YOU. YOU are the Originator of every beautiful thing in my life. I bless you for the continual "opening of my eyes," and the desire to Shift into greater Newness "when I've recognized that my place of convenience has become obsolete!" Expanding in my love for you in every moment..

Mom & Dad; You're both with God now, but I feel and remember YOU everyday. I didn't understand in the beginning. But I do now. Forever love…

Bridget, and our three amigos Benjamin, Loren, and Zion; We started this Journey to the Amazing over 20 years ago. Years of teaching ourselves as we drove in the car or went on walks. The constant miracles together while we lived in California. The many "lost books" along the way, even the "brushes with death we encountered in the desert!" We are living the most incredible life, regardless of the "challenges of inspiration" we've encountered together. We each have been given the gift of "Change and Purpose!" I'm thankful to God that you all have allowed me to "explore the depths of my Person," even when it came to a great sacrifice to your time and presence. You are teaching me so much on HOW to BE! I am truly blessed for the years. I LOVE YOU! "And I think y'all love me too!" :-)

Myles Munroe and Wilson Douglass III; You both have challenged me as a Spirit and as a Man! I am forever grateful to the both of YOU!

Krystal and Journey; The world is yours. Go get it! I love the both of you...

Tracy Mac; Continue in your life's call. You are a wonderful friend in this Path of Enlightenment! You've done it Chick!

Van Smith; you've been such an incredible encourager, mercy giver, listening ear, resource, and companion. But most of all, you've been a son and friend. Love you so much.

Paul, Thomas, Steve, and my friends at Peli Peli; Thanks for giving me the room to explore my musical creativity and life experience. I thank you for pushing me beyond my creative limits. Thanks for the "teaching" without teaching. Thanks for the smiles and the laughter. Thank you for believing and prospering me. Thank you for what you've added to my life. I love and appreciate you all.

All of my Universal and KAIROS family; Thank you for supporting me through the years. Forgive me when it seemed that I didn't understand or considered your feelings. I have always loved you and wanted the best for you. Thank you for your years of assistance, laughter, and resources to help me along the way. I only pray that YOU too, received a treasure within you for working with me! I could not have done anything without you. Well, maybe I could have, "but YOU all made it more worthwhile being together!" You added a flavor to it that I could not have experienced alone! I love you all!

Kim Bady; Thank you for the belief. Thank you for the love. Thank you for dancing! LOL! Let's do this again, ok?

Foreword

We all live with a foundation, seen or unseen, of silent principles that propel us. The question very well may be where are our principles directing us to or toward? Attempting to answer that question could lead us to ask ourselves some of the most important questions...What is my purpose? Why am I here?

And although we all have asked ourselves these questions, the truths that are written inside this book were not designed to give you your answer(s), but more so to help you to eliminate unnecessary thought patterns that could've very well kept you from finding your own answers before now. This is not only a lifestyle change, but a mind-style change. Change the way you think and everything after that must follow.

This change of thinking will direct or re-direct your life so that you can not only see yourself and for yourself, but to also aid you to be clear and focused on where you are going in your own personal Path.

So I ask you to look forward...look ahead. Allow these writings to propel the intelligence of YOU and cause you to really recognize the power to Be.

Dr. Bridget Fizer, The KAIROS Institute

INTRODUCTION

I decided to write this "daily compass" to aid you in the furtherance of your personal, and even spiritual enlightenment," because it's something that I wished was in existence when I was inspired to "find and embrace" my true Self! I am giving you "what I wish I had" when I was living in this same place as you! I am sharing my Mind and my Discoveries with you. And believe me, there is so much more to all of US! I am sharing a "few thoughts" with you and I expect that the few thoughts you will read in this book "will awaken a myriad of Thoughts within YOU too!"

This is a Great Moment for all of US! We are living in the most incredible time in our lives. And the BEST is already within YOU! Let's see what we'll create together.

Be open. Don't fear. You'll probably be surprised at everything You'll discover about YOU. I am merely assisting you in the "opening of your eyes," but how YOU respond to "the LIGHT" is completely up to your own tolerance!

I've entitled the book "365" because we've all been given the gift of EVERYDAY to become NEW, and every moment to realize that there is "so much more to BE!" EVERYDAY. EVERY MOMENT! 365 days a year!

Are you ready?

SECTIONS

Affirmations Part I:
THE JOURNEY TO AWARENESS

INTRODUCTION

I wonder what it was that "sparked" your curiosity; the object that captivated your soul to the point of even "considering" a move beyond your familiar place of life. What were you, or are you, expecting to find? Discover? Recover? Have you determined what it is you're looking for? Do you feel lost without it?

Desires to venture out into the "unfamiliar" are nestled deep within the confines of every soul, "but only few ever gain the confidence or the boldness" to chart a course to this very beautiful kingdom that resides within the corridors of our very own spirit! What is it that inspires an individual to "forsake" what they've comfortably known "as truth" for years and "to explore a Depth of Understanding that may not be easily attainable, or even true for that matter?" However, it was "true enough" to awaken a curiosity within you, and shed light to a "path" you've never seen before, but believe with all of your heart, "that it's there!"

Once the fear of the unexpected, or the anxieties of abandonment have been eradicated or better yet, "held captive," the Door will open to this incredible horizon called "YOU!" Then, you will begin to realize what a beautifully intelligent and divine being you truly are.

And the Thoughts begin NOW!

Your "Life" will treat YOU according to the degree YOU feel your presence means to it; the same way! According to your faith "will everything BE to YOU!" Shift Your Faith, Shift Your World....

:: ::

Give Yourself the same respect You would give to others who are seen as the Affluent of this World! Always applaud and celebrate Your presence in this world. You are not a "backdrop" in the Universe, but a significant piece to the landscape!

:: ::

Bring peace to "your world" by allowing Peace in Yourself! Make no room for the darkness of foolishness in Your "Divine Community!" You were designed to "keep the LIGHT ON" in your Temple!

:: ::

It is not a prideful or arrogant thing "to BE the BEST YOU!" Glory feared "is glory stolen!" Glory embraced is the Pleasure of God!

:: ::

Never lessen the Power of Your Existence by conditioning Yourself "to never Arrive!" If the Journey picked YOU up at the Port of Decision, surely it must "dock" somewhere!

:: ::

If YOU "knew that there was a billion dollars" in an account for YOU, YOU would not BE where YOU are right NOW! Unknown Choices and Decisions are like hidden money. If YOU knew where those greater Decisions were located, YOU WOULD BE SOMEPLACE ELSE in your life and Mind! Search Your Spirit! Silent ignorance of Decision "will leave YOU where YOU are!"

:: ::

Silent "ignorance" will rob YOU of an Eternal Shift, while leaving you with the "crumbs of the moment!" What YOU have right NOW "may not be all YOU were intended to have!" Search Your Spirit, for within it are the Greater Choices and Decisions!"

:: ::

"Re-Covering Your Originality is dangerous to the health of your intimidation!"

:: ::

Everyone of US "were Pleasures to Create!"

:: ::

Fear isn't "obligated" to be the "official", initial feeling You experience when facing New Frontiers and Opportunities of Life!

:: ::

YOU are what God came up with "after a discussion with Himself!" What will YOU create after a "discussion with Yourself?" You are the DAY you make....

:: ::

If it's possible for God to have a belief system, "It would have to be LOVE" and nothing else! Forgiveness is Divine Love "overwhelming the sting of death in every area of life and consciousness!"

:: ::

Every second of life "YOU become a New Creation" while learning to articulate The Experience! YOU are "arriving and leaving" at the same time! And becoming a Master "when YOU remember!"

:: ::

God is so amazing that HE lives "beyond the bible!" In order to discover all of HIM "you must look within ALL OF YOU!" Believe me, He won't be offended if You do!

:: ::

As soon as YOU say "YES" or "I understand" to Possibility, it suddenly takes control of the Day without your permission, neither is it considerate of your feelings or pace of life!

:: ::

Religion is too small for YOU, as well as an insult to your

Intelligence. NOW is the time "to see who YOU truly are, as well as how expansive YOU can truly love!"

:: ::

We all possess a Divine Spark "that has never failed at any Time!"

:: ::

When You've been "Caught" Your life and Mind won't wander all over the Place. An "uncaught soul" will tire itself out, looking for things "that are already present within!"

:: ::

Allow the essence of Goodness to breathe within YOU! It may not bring everything Your temporal desires may crave, but surely, It will bring Food for the Soul! It will make YOU ALIVE!

:: ::

If your "dreams" are competing against someone else, then You're in the wrong game "because You're the only ONE who's supposed to be here!"

:: ::

Allow Yourself to become more than "smart on paper!" Your Dreams desire to take YOU somewhere higher in YOU! C'mon, get in this "Game of One!"

:: ::

What will WE create today? Take your Peace of Mind and create "Peace of Life and Peace of Action!"

:: ::

The Moment YOU begin to "feel" what YOU have hoped for is the Moment YOU can begin to bring it to Reality! What you have longed for will let YOU know that "it's alive" when it touches your feelings. And we all have the Power to call forth Every living Thing, even if they are invisible to the eye!

:: ::

There is something that is "attracting" YOU to "live different, think different, and become a difference!" Learn the art of articulating your Divine Frequencies. Give it an identity. Slow down and Define it. Learn it. Speak to it. Become it...

:: ::

Others believing in YOU "is strictly optional!" YOU, believing not only in Yourself, but in the Reason YOU were sent to this world, is NOT!

:: ::

It's not impossible, neither complicated. You can "become it!"

:: ::

Is "this" a Powerful MOMENT for YOU "RIGHT NOW?" If not, what are YOU willing to do "to create one?"

:: ::

The Results we desire are easy to pray for. But the "ways" to the Results are usually "attacked" by our fear of Change and the Experience of "Unfamiliar Movement!"

:: ::

The Results we so desperately crave and seek after are usually byproducts of "habits and instructions we despise or make excuses for not doing!" In order to reside in the Result "we must honor the Seed that created it!"

:: ::

When YOU truly trust Your heart "YOU will give Your life to Your Beliefs!"

:: ::

How possible do YOU "want" to BE? Allow yourself the right to become everything YOU want to be "without the fear of thinking it's wrong!"

:: ::

YOU can have it "if you're willing to be misjudged for it, despised for it, held accountable to it, and questioned about it." If you can endure the hate for possessing it, you've deemed yourself worthy to receive all of the Love, Power, and Mastery for obtaining it! Are YOU worthy to be YOU?

:: ::

An "awakening" despised is "ignorance loved!" Awakenings mature into Constant Evolution only "when the participant makes their residence there!" But when the − "familiar is a friend," the light of the Awakening becomes a dimly lit memory of the past...

:: ::

When Your "life's hunger" is to give the Unlimited Good, The Divine will remove the "hinges from every door" that seemingly stood in your way, and will grant YOU access to the entire Universe!

:: ::

Since You're going to do what YOU want to do anyway, "why not make it Great, Memorable, and Powerful!" Inspire the World to ask for an Encore!

:: ::

There will arrive within You, a Divine Moment of Power, that is not meant to be bottled up and presented as a sermon or testimony for church, but as an expression of the Love and Healing to those who exist in the world! YOU were never created for what YOU can do on Sundays, but for who YOU are to be "in the world!"

:: ::

Imagine fulfillment until it makes YOU laugh on the Inside! Imagine bringing healing to another "till it makes YOU tingle with Pleasure!" The Atmosphere will "tilt" because of it "and bring this Opportunity to your Life!"

:: ::

Within all of us, beneath the experiences of pain, and our respected, familiar concepts of life, is a sound "in the form of a feeling!" If we listen with our heart, it will "lead us to The Door!" It is the FIRST SOUND you ever heard, "and this is why we call it Our First Mind!"

:: ::

Torment is when you know more than you're willing to do! The Miraculous is when you've done more "than you've ever known!"

:: ::

Hey YOU! Wherever YOU are in "your world" today, know that I desire for YOU To DO the Best YOU can. And if Change of any kind is in order, go beyond your fear and embrace it. See if there is something "BEYOND" where YOU are. And if YOU want it, "GO GET IT!" Peace...

:: ::

I found that my "daily world" functions to the degree in which I have truly recognized the Power and Relevance of my Divine Self. I don't "live" in the world. I AM "my world!" You are "your World!"

:: ::

YOU possess the Power to affirm Your own Significance in the world. The Divine has already affirmed Your Importance by your existence. But it is up to YOU to affirm Your existence "by your actions". Live Important!

:: ::

The Universe awaits our constant contributions of Love, Thought, and Discovery. The Galaxies possess more than enough room for everyone of us "to fill it with the essence of the Divine!" We all are "the lights of worlds!" No one is obligated "to be blind!"

:: ::

Have YOU determined if "the Divine Consciousness" is necessary for YOU to achieve the Quality of life you so desperately desire? Have you determined the "value of your life's Path?" How much will YOU invest in it? What will it take to "acquire" what YOU desire?

:: ::

Truth does not disconnect US from Pleasure. It disconnects US from "the desires of everything that is lifeless!" The fullness of life and Mind "is unmeasurable Pleasure, Passion, and Purpose!"

In order to receive "the unusual" YOU must first live and practice "the Unusual," meaning "don't be surprised if you're misunderstood, unsupported, or left standing by yourself!" This is what You asked for. So, you must commit to the Path of the Unusual Blessing!

:: ::

Stop thinking that "you're crazy" when Unusual Truths or Ideas are breeding within Your spirit. You're a genius. And stop allowing the balance in your bank account to tell you otherwise. That too, will change! You already have enough "to BEGIN!"

:: ::

Don't make changes "because" you're 18. Don't make changes "because" you're in your 30's, 40's, or even 50's. Do it because "it's Time!" Do it because "You're Alive!"

:: ::

Whatever YOU are most at peace "with" will create Peace "for" YOU daily. You'd be surprised at the number of individuals who are most at peace "with fear, ignorance, and the familiar!" You determine "the quality of your daily experiences and discoveries!"

:: ::

Vision will require the acquisition of new life and Emotional Skills. Spirituality, in order to be profoundly relevant, must move us into new spheres of global life comprehension and mastery! It must also compel us to embrace new spheres of Thought and Imagination. This is where our "inner leadership" begins…

:: ::

Relationships may feel complicated "when the Divine compels it to go beyond talk" and into oneness/trust/love! When it causes us to "move Beyond the familiar" and into our Consciousness of life. Begin the Journey of Allowance. Let yourself "embrace Peace" during this "Uncertainty!"

:: ::

You will naturally "move forward" when "the space" that occupies your "habit and thought" has become "too uncomfortable" to tolerate! The need to "break the walls" of perception will become inevitable!

:: ::

If YOU live the Path of the Decisions that YOU are needing to make, "YOU won't be overwhelmed by the significance of them!" The "flow of Your life" is a natural manifestation of "moment by moment" decisions YOU are consistently making! Peace…

:: ::

Possibilities and Impossibilities "are both offsprings" of how we view the validity of our own existence in this world! They are not "handed" to YOU from another! YOU do have the permission to BE "whatever YOU are ready to endure!"

:: ::

Are you getting closer to who YOU desire to BE? Follow your JOY "because happiness can fool YOU if you're not careful!" Peace...

:: ::

Take those "déjà vu" moments YOU are experiencing "and begin to prepare for a NEW SHIFT!" Whenever YOU experience a Moment when you say "I've seen this before," it is the Divine's way of telling YOU to "Evaluate Your Happenings, reconsider Your Path, and embrace the opportunities that will spark a New Habit within YOU!" Bless YOU!

:: ::

Destiny has mentored YOU for years in the form of "childlike imaginations, invisible playmates, and endless wonderment!" It now mentors YOU into the form of an innate "dissatisfaction of the status quo, the familiar, and the mundane!" Are YOU ready to AWAKEN who You've always been? You've been "watched" for Years "by the things YOU have yet to perform!"

:: ::

My Humanity loves the Power of my Divinity "while my Divinity is loving how it positions the daily momentum of my Humanity!" When God created us "the first thing He did was speak to Himself!" We too, can do the same! My humanity loves when my Divinity "speaks!"

:: ::

No relationship should put an end to YOU "being YOU!" Life's biggest tragedy is the annihilation of Originality! It's even bigger when the annihilator is YOU!

:: ::

The more excellent Manifestations of Life are created by those who've grown tired and offended with "thinking only!"

:: ::

One day, when YOU wake up in the morning, YOU will find yourself taking a ... drive to your PLEASURE instead of maneuvering the vehicle in order to park "where you despise!" HOW? Live Necessary! Think Necessary! Love what's Necessary! Practice what's Necessary! BE what's Necessary! Don't give "Waste" a reason to be a friend...

:: ::

Understanding of a lot of things will come the Moment "You put YOURSELF out there!" If someone else is "putting you out there," you won't comprehend a thing! When VISION awakens, "your present room of life" will instantly become "too small," and YOU will "break the Walls all by yourself!"

:: ::

When You're "ready" you will no longer plague yourselves with the "constant inner questions of uncertainty and of missing God!" Sometimes, the "what ifs" are more tormenting than the actual movement itself. When you're ready "no one will find YOU where they used to find YOU!"

:: ::

Okay, the "problems' been identified, and all of the issues have been given a name and a strategy!" NOW WHAT? Sometimes, the problems are not people, God, pastors, religion, or any such thing. Sometimes, the issue is "we're not ready!" Greatness can be so inconvenient "when you're not ready!"

:: ::

You must accept the fact that this world isn't relevant without YOU! So, now that YOU know this, "plant your Best of Mind into the fabric of this Atmosphere!" Don't live "missing" while Visible!

:: ::

Make sure You're on your own "friends list!" You're going to need "YOU" more than YOU think! Live Profound today!

:: ::

Only Create those things "you desire to go through!" Oh, it's possible alright. Just look at the causes and issues behind what YOU went through last "and ask yourself the hard questions surrounding the circumstances!" NOW, live and do differently!

:: ::

You will constantly "attract" what You're constantly ready to do! Those who win "will attract Opportunities that maximize." Those who employ excuse will attract "obligation that will justify the need for excuse!"

:: ::

YOU and I are "acts" of God. A "mighty act" I might say! The Atmosphere is praising the both of us as we speak. I'm not "arrogant," just divinely relevant...

:: ::

The Divine never presents Opportunities when you're prepared for them, but when "your life is entrenched in everything else that has nothing to do with the Opportunity!" Is "right now" too soon?

:: ::

More of God "is still too little!" Less of YOU "is still too much!" ONENESS, SAMENESS, "brings the Calm, destroys the torments of seeking," and lights the Whole World! Oneness it is...

:: ::

The reason "all hell" breaks loose when YOU decide to live your Original Self is because "hell" is where you were living before you came to your Decision! Hell "isn't breaking loose!" ALL of YOU is "breaking OUT!" "Hell" is no longer "your apartment!"

:: ::

A "true Awakening" will never allow the "comforts of obsolete, or misinterpreted revelation" to exist within your Consciousness! It will never allow YOU to "remain enslaved" for "a friend!"

:: ::

The NEW thing that YOU keep saying You're going to BE "will do everything It can to make sure that your comfort zones stop liking YOU in hopes of securing Your release!"

:: ::

In spite of what "peaks your interests," YOU will only live "what YOU have given yourself permission to live!" Your efforts will never exceed beyond your point of intrigue. You are wherever You've stopped," or wherever You're continuing to evolve!" Your life isn't obligated to have a finish line!

:: ::

JOY is a Gift that your soul will never accept from anyone else "but YOU!" So, you can stop frustrating your life with that long wait! No one else has it in their possession, "nor do they know where to find it!"

:: ::

Whatever is Yours "will call out to You daily!" Sometimes, Purpose isn't found in what YOU see yourself doing, but in what YOU "see yourself answering!"

:: ::

The fluidity, intensity, creativity, and wisdom of Your life is a direct reflection of the Object your soul "is divinely intimate with!" YOU are the likeness "of what YOU like!"

:: ::

If whatever You're living for "can die," then you have not yet discovered Your Purpose! When you live for something that cannot die, "You won't either!"

:: ::

When everyday life is "common, mundane, and average," You will find it constantly "diffusing the spark of an Inspired Thought!" NOW is the time to "fuse" your Excitement and your life together to form an Incredible Partnership of Reality! Are YOU ready to "create the Chance?"

:: ::

It may be unfamiliar, but it's not Impossible! It will become your friend in a minute!

:: ::

The "motives" that produced your incredible ideas will determine "if and when" those Ideas are "attempted or accomplished!" The "right WHY" will empower You to stay the Course while the "common Why" will have you living as a "chameleon, changing and adapting to whoever or whatever You're with, without BECOMING anything significant or whole!"

:: ::

Incompetence! Are YOU living what YOU desire, or what You HAVE TO?

:: ::

You "become" what You condition yourself for! Stop conditioning yourself for "an attack" and begin to condition yourself for Clear Paths to Completeness!

:: ::

We must never become addicted to "our own sounds of unpracticed Wisdom" to the point "we fear the actual DOING of those Great Things we've said and thought!"

:: ::

"Oneness with God" gives me the permission to ignore "the devil and his little self" as long as I desire!

:: ::

Keep "unfolding" Yourselves until the Places YOU actually "see" with Your "eyes" are the exact Places that reside within Your Soul! And then evolve again "even the more!" Those "feelings" you have within are actually connected to something "Out There and In Here!"

:: ::

The "fear of Your Glory" will keep YOU from loving all of YOU, and others from loving "all of YOU" too! There is soooo much of US "that we must learn to love!" Divine

Image feared "is a destruction invited!" You must remember that YOU are the Glory of God! He isn't threatened by the discovery of it!

:: ::

It's not "what" You think but "HOW" You think that will determine if YOU are ready to participate with the Miraculous!

:: ::

Hello Incredible Mind. Refrain from the fear of Wholeness! Those who have been "wounded much" will seek to control "outcomes much!" The relinquishment of control "is the beginning of Oneness!"

:: ::

When you're in love with The Path "the Walk will naturally reveal itself to YOU!"

:: ::

Intentionally develop mindsets, disciplines, and habits that will make it impossible for your life to get "stuck!" Our habits can launch us into incredible horizons or either hold us hostage to what we've always seen and been!

:: ::

YOU, "are the best that God could do!" He's not still working on YOU! He's done. But there is a Moment arriving, and it may have already showed up, when YOU will recognize "what He's already finished!"

:: ::

Something as simple as an "argument" can determine how much, or if, "you have truly evolved!" Arguments reveal "the present state of desire, disappointment, and even the validity of one's purpose in life and relationship!" Arguments reveal "what certain works will not," which is TRUTH! Evolution of Spirit has many faces. Don't be afraid of it!

:: ::

Have YOU "risen" from the "grave of doubt, fear, intimidation, procrastination, disinterest of Self, Identity, and Purpose, excuse, inner poverty, obligation, inner-religion, and unworthiness?" Which of the "3" days are YOU "yet stuck in?" Live "risen" in Mind, Body, and Spirit!

:: ::

Confidence confirms that intimidation is absent from the soul!

:: ::

Most of us never really learn from our mistakes. We're just grateful that we were able to live to make another! Real, huh? Focus. Listen. Become. Overcome. Live "what YOU want to SEE!"

:: ::

Within YOU is a Divine Intuition which is commonly called "SOMETHING told me!" Well, that "Something" never stops speaking. Allow it to be an intricate part of your life Scheme! God isn't embarrassed "if you didn't call Him God!" He usually dwells within the confines of "intuition, feeling, thought, and that little nerve that agitates YOU until YOU do something different!"

:: ::

You will DO the Will of whatever YOU desire to be Guided by the most! Your "dominant guide" determines the Pathways of Your life, Mind, and Energy!

:: ::

Don't insult your self-encouragement by "preparing Your heart to fail!"

:: ::

Beneath all of the years of obligatory thinking, abuse, self-hatred, arrogance, fear of Success and fear of failure, manipulation and deception from yourself and others, sickness, poverty, evictions and foreclosures, secrets, shame, and hopelessness, "is a Divine Identity waiting to shine and bring light to Your Path on the Real!" Unearth "the Flow!"

:: ::

Believe me, all of the "desires" YOU have that are positive, impacting, powerful and empowering, are not keeping YOU hostage to the misery YOU may be experiencing now!

So, "who's keeping YOU?" Is it the fear of Responsibility? Or, the fear of leaving the familiar "and never going back to visit?" Sometimes, the answers are more intimidating than the misery!

:: ::

Misery and Unhappiness is not a result of what others have done to YOU, but the result of "letting them" do it! It's also the result of the Divine that You have "not allowed" Yourself to BE!

:: ::

Your DIVINITY isn't favor. It isn't a reward for being "good!" It just "IS!" Just flow with The FLOW of it and watch it take YOU to many places within YOU that " YOU never even heard of!"

:: ::

God can't change YOU "if YOU already like what YOU are!"

WHAT RESONATED WITH YOU
ABOUT THIS CHAPTER?

WHAT WAS YOUR "KEY WORD OR THOUGHT" FROM THIS CHAPTER?

_____

_____

_____

_____

_____

_____

_____

_____

_____

_____

_____

_____

_____

_____

_____

_____

_____

WHAT ARE YOU GOING TO DO NOW?

_____

_____

_____

_____

_____

_____

_____

_____

_____

_____

_____

_____

_____

_____

_____

_____

_____

_____

_____

WHEN WILL YOU GET STARTED?

_____

_____

_____

_____

_____

_____

_____

_____

_____

_____

_____

_____

_____

_____

_____

_____

_____

_____

_____

_____

WHY HAVEN'T YOU STARTED?

_____

_____

_____

_____

_____

_____

_____

_____

_____

_____

_____

_____

_____

_____

_____

_____

_____

_____

_____

_____

_____

Affirmations Part II:
WHO ARE YOU REALLY?

.

INTRODUCTION

I'm going to ask you a question.

How do you feel "being YOU?" In the midst of this vast universe, have you defined how you feel about YOU "being here?" How do you see the world? How do You see "You" in the world "you see?" Where do you fit? Are YOU being "heard and understood?"

Have you determined your "validity" in this universe? Where do you belong? What Purpose do you serve in being here? What do you really feel in your heart?

Significance and Authenticity of Life are two of the most incredibly "boldest" things you can discover about yourself, for an authentic life is a constant threat to the "comforts of human acceptance!" When you arrive to this realization, you will have discovered that you are "the greatest thought that God ever had, or will have, in His Life!"

And the Thoughts begin NOW!

YOU are living both as Human and Divine. Live magnificently, significantly, and purposeful, "in both!" Jesus did.

:: ::

God doesn't have time "to dislike YOU!"

:: ::

When YOU "become" in the NOW "who YOU have always existed as since the Beginnings of Time, the earth "will yield her strength to YOU!" Embrace and Live from the Identity "that causes Atmospheres to explode with Resources of Significance towards YOU!"

:: ::

You are "what YOU think" YOU are. YOU are not obligated to confirm the inferior, or even positive opinions of another. Who do YOU "think" YOU are? Have you defined your "image" in this world?

:: ::

How "ONE" are YOU willing to BE? Multiple frustrations are attracted to those who live "as Many!"

:: ::

I Am...enough!

:: ::

When you "see Yourself," is there a "spark" that tells your heart that YOU are "looking at God?" We lose the essence of our Identity "when God remains someone we can never see, or ever be!"

:: ::

Impossible to lose "sight" of God when you're living and seeing from within HIM! You're no longer looking for something already FOUND, but seeking to give what YOU FOUND to the World. I live, seeking people while creating Divine Opportunities to release all of the Fullness of Who and What I have found. Looking for God is not the Goal anymore. I AM what God is, seeking the world!

:: ::

Live Profound! You will never stop people from "talking," BUT you can definitely "shut off their volume" by Being Your Original YOU, even amidst the worst that can be said about YOU! YOU must BECOME the GREATER SOUND!

:: ::

The views and opinions YOU fear the most "are the ones that own Your heart, mind, and future!" They also own the views YOU have of Yourself! YOU must embrace the Boldness in leading Yourself into the realities and rewards of Personal and Spiritual Discoveries!

:: ::

YOU are "the world" you're changing. Become "everything to life" that YOU desire to see. Become the love that you desire to feel, as well as the Mercy you desire to experience..

:: ::

Our "flaws" are not of imperfection, but are the "exit wounds" from which we were all "taken from one another" and brought to this world. If YOU look closely at God, You will see "that He has an exit wound" as well. We all "are Perfect" indeed! We ALL carry the "marks" of Uniqueness and Oneness...

:: ::

I AM "what my beliefs" Believe... And my life's habit will manifest the Quality of that belief without struggle, "regardless if they're good or bad!"

:: ::

God "is not tolerating us" through Jesus. He "knows" US. He "knows" Me! I AM "as He is," in this world...

:: ::

Within YOU is a "Team of Resources, Ideas, and Timefulness" that are ready to assist YOU if You're ready! YOU will make it happen "when YOU can handle it WHEN it Happens!"

:: ::

You were born with a natural, uninhibited way of celebrating the existence of God and Self until religious misunderstanding came along and gave us a citation for BEING! Don't worry though. That dictatorship has been overturned. Resume to Innocence, The Creative, and the True. Live Divine "in the face of the law!"

:: ::

Whatever I worship "will give me all of its strength and thought!" If I worship procrastination, it will protect me from being "moved to action" when Opportunity arrives! If I worship Transformation, I will gravitate to every "purposeful opportunity that arises, even if unfamiliar!" My daily reality is a reflection of what the soul worships much!

:: ::

Just because God "created" Us doesn't necessarily mean that His Consciousness is "fathering us!" Our daily reality of "naturalness and spiritualness" is a reflection of what is truly "fathering" our Consciousness!

:: ::

You are only as Powerful and Whole "as the Love you're loving with!"

:: ::

You and satan "are NOT the same people!" Believe me, God can surely tell the difference!

:: ::

We and God, God and Us, "are the same People!" Peace!

:: ::

Fear will let YOU wear God's "shoes," but Oneness will let you share His feet. Oneness will give YOU what YOU can't "take off!"

:: ::

If you devote the bulk of your energy to things you don't have to do, then "what you didn't have to do" will steal "what you had to do!" Protecting your time wisely will protect your life's Purpose! Determine within yourself to commit to the right affairs of life.

:: ::

We all reflect everything our soul is in love with. Love, regardless of the quality of the object, will express the Object in ways that reveal the nature of the Object. If hatred is loved perfectly, it will hurt YOU! If goodness is loved perfectly, it will "heal YOU!" Love gives all of our "hidden residence of Thought" a "feeling, an emotion and life!" What is Your Soul loving "from?"

:: ::

WE are the "confirmers" of The Divine Existence! WE are the LIFE of the Divine...

:: ::

Never grant someone else "the initial opinion" of YOU! Let them think whatever they want "but make sure the truth of YOU is with YOU!"

:: ::

God has always been "one of US!"

:: ::

What makes Jesus so cool "is that He always made YOU feel cool too!" His "spirituality" treated everyone "as though they were already ok!" All He ever did was "re-connect the Family!"

WHAT RESONATED WITH YOU
ABOUT THIS CHAPTER?

_____

_____

_____

_____

_____

_____

_____

_____

_____

_____

_____

_____

_____

_____

_____

_____

_____

_____

_____

_____

_____

What Was Your "KEY WORD or THOUGHT" from this Chapter?

_____

_____

_____

_____

_____

_____

_____

_____

_____

_____

_____

_____

_____

_____

_____

_____

_____

_____

_____

What Are YOU Going To Do NOW?

_____

_____

_____

_____

_____

_____

_____

_____

_____

_____

_____

_____

_____

_____

_____

_____

_____

WHEN WILL YOU GET STARTED?

_____

_____

_____

_____

_____

_____

_____

_____

_____

_____

_____

_____

_____

_____

_____

_____

_____

_____

_____

Why Haven't YOU Started?

_____

_____

_____

_____

_____

_____

_____

_____

_____

_____

_____

_____

_____

_____

_____

_____

_____

_____

_____

Affirmations Part III:
MORE POWERFUL THAN WE'VE IMAGINED

INTRODUCTION

Really, what are you afraid of? Success? Failure? Both?

Have you determined the type of influence you possess? Not influence over other people, but "the Invisible?" Does Life "listen to YOU?" Does LIFE "respect" your existence in the world? How does LIFE feel about YOU being here, alive and well? Does LIFE anticipate your waking up each morning? Does LIFE yearn to learn "about your thoughts, wisdom, and solutions?"

Do you believe that you're this powerful? This influential? This Significant? This important? If you don't believe it in your soul "you will not embrace it in your mind!" You will become a victim of constant circumstance, and the torment of anticipated failures!

But this doesn't have to be so. Allow yourself to be important to the world. Allow yourself to feel worthy enough to share the essence of the Divine Mind in this world! You are an offspring of the Divine Intelligence, and a possessor of the Greatest Gene of Power in this world and beyond!

And the Thoughts begin NOW!

We will not be able to change anything that we "silently feel" has a "sacred right to exist!" Your WORDS will create "when you remove the legal right of existence" of the things YOU seek to SHIFT from Your Consciousness!

:: ::

You are the Master to things that obey YOU the most "and the servant to those things that won't!" Define your "audience!" It's not impossible!

:: ::

Your LIFE will change whenever You're ready! Until then, everything else is an excuse! Embrace the Power in "Being the MOMENT!"

:: ::

Are YOU READY to BE "what YOU need THIS MOMENT to BE," right NOW? What do we need to do?

:: ::

You're "more than able" if YOU allow yourself to be. It's only impossible "when you don't allow Possibility to mentor YOU!" You can do ANYTHING if you're willing to learn EVERYTHING you need to accomplish it!

:: ::

Within YOU "are all the People YOU need to get it done!"

:: ::

Know that "every THING" has transcended possible today! ALL is DO-ABLE, DONE, and awaiting a Command from YOU right NOW!

:: ::

Don't be afraid. Send YOUR Word "to the whatevers" in Your life and expect them to align! Determine "how your world SHOULD view YOU" and live accordingly! Expect Harmony…

:: ::

Every second is an opportunity for YOU to "create again!" We do more "than try!" WE BE! So never let your seconds become days. Give an assignment to every second of YOUR LIFE!

:: ::

LIFE "will be" whatever YOU ARE!

:: ::

Your life will obey "whomever" You do!

:: ::

Expecting everyone with a "womb of Promise" to experience the ultimate Purpose of themselves, the fullness of God within themselves, and Original Intention that inspired their creations. Desiring for every Woman, mother or not, to take their glimpses of Greatness "and expand them into

Full Expressions of DIVINE LIFE!" You are so much more "than Eve!" Love YOU!

:: ::

You don't need a miracle. Just an opportunity! BE NOW, LIVE NOW, "what YOU would do, when YOU GET IT!" The POWER is always in NOW!

:: ::

Life responds, not according to what YOU say, but according to who YOU "feel" You truly are!

:: ::

Distractions aren't always "surprises!" Sometimes, purposely devoting positive energy to things that are of no purpose at all "are distractions!" Time gone!

:: ::

Go on and live free "everywhere!"

:: ::

Never allow your misery to enlarge itself beyond the LOVE that is capable of healing it. God "still loves the world!"

:: ::

Never choose "who or what" to forgive! When you release Love and New Beginnings to "everything," EVERYTHING will grant new beginnings to YOU without prejudice or judgment! This is so incredible to live!

:: ::

To some, it's easier to give "principles" you do not practice yourself, to a stranger than to a friend. For to be "a new person" in front of a stranger "is not truly being NEW at all!" BECOME an Authenticity that can stand on it's own anywhere and with anyone!

:: ::

The Divine you are "isn't considering where it will spend Eternity!" It's already existing from it!

:: ::

Divine intelligence naturally creates what is Intelligent! You have the right to trust Your LIFE! There is no "ignorant gene" within YOU! You are walking Intelligence! Evolving Wisdom and "right NOW Truth!" Trust it. Listen to it "because it can listen to YOU!"

WHAT RESONATED WITH YOU
ABOUT THIS CHAPTER?

_____

_____

_____

_____

_____

_____

_____

_____

_____

_____

_____

_____

_____

_____

_____

_____

_____

_____

_____

WHAT WAS YOUR "KEY WORD OR THOUGHT"
FROM THIS CHAPTER?

_____

_____

_____

_____

_____

_____

_____

_____

_____

_____

_____

_____

_____

_____

_____

_____

_____

_____

_____

_____

WHAT ARE YOU GOING TO DO NOW?

WHEN WILL YOU GET STARTED?

_____

_____

_____

_____

_____

_____

_____

_____

_____

_____

_____

_____

_____

_____

_____

_____

_____

_____

_____

WHY HAVEN'T YOU STARTED?

_____

_____

_____

_____

_____

_____

_____

_____

_____

_____

_____

_____

_____

_____

_____

_____

_____

_____

_____

Affirmations Part IV
SHATTERING THE ILLUSIONS

INTRODUCTION

You'd be surprised at how much we sabotage our own lives by believing things "that never arrived, never lived, and never can be!" Lies, that appear to be "true!" This is what we call "illusions!" The appearance of something that may exist, but really is the figment of our own, distorted imagination. And to add insult to injury, some of these "truths" are things we have "borrowed" from the fears of other people.

As you move forward in the recovery of your Divine LIFE, you will find yourself "shattering the illusions" that have guided your life, "sincerely," for years. You will find yourself breaking free from self-imposed limitations and "truths" that were responsible for the formation of your "personality, lifestyle, and opinions!" And you will begin to "introduce yourself" to YOURSELF within every moment you are privileged to experience!

Just watch!

And the Thoughts begin NOW!

The "religious world" was not created by God, but is a byproduct of our misunderstanding...

:: ::

You are only as amazing "as the worthiness YOU feel within Yourself!" Struggles are the natural results of feeling unworthy, even when the unworthiness is "resting silently!"

:: ::

An "unpracticed" inspirational message will not Inspire! Practice the Inspiration and you will go farther "than the nod of agreement!"

:: ::

Believe it or not, this world was designed for the NOW "Lordship of Us!" Raise more than your thinking. Raise Your LIFE!

:: ::

Not only do You have the capacity to comprehend, with ease, out of this world Truth, YOU also have the ability to live them with ease!

:: ::

If we have to tell ourselves "that it's alright to live, laugh, and love," then we have allowed Religion to inject us with destruction, and the misinterpretation of God to be our compass!

:: ::

If I live from LOVE "you will never have to worry about ME creating something lawless, destructive, or despicable!" When WE are LOVE, "the laws that regulate creativity" are lifted, and WE are given "the keys to the Mind of Ourselves as God!" It is only when we feel "despicable" that we "fear what we may create!"

:: ::

Conclusions that produce no responsible action, will only further the "present confusion!" Arriving to conclusions, without the implementation of action, is "not enough!" God blesses the Action that precedes the Conclusion! Move on!

:: ::

There is no need to "fear" the Pleasures of Goodness, Hope, and Fulfilled Dreams! You're not being "set Up" to learn a lesson from failure and disappointment! When the "shadows of Goodness" overtakes Your presence, Abandon Yourself in the light that is producing it!

:: ::

How is it, "when peril" hits the world, it is so easy to point to the Bible in order to confirm "the end of all things!" But when Love, Hope, Purpose, and Awareness is constantly shared, it is seen "as a cloak from the devil," blinding the minds of those who desire to see life from a Higher Consciousness? Is Death, Destruction, and Darkness so much "greater" than love, Soundness, and life?

:: ::

"Sin" should never be the thing that we are most assured of committing in our lives. Failure "should never be a given," while Winning and living a life of Significance is considered "a process!" Our Humanity has been conditioned of an "assurance of failure" as long as we live in it, instead of an assurance of Incredible Possibilities. Change Your Mind!

:: ::

YOU are "already delivered from evil!" NOW, you are facing the realities of Decision and Choice!

:: ::

What "we do" with Words of God "will determine what God does" through our Words!

:: ::

Words only have Power "when YOU believe them!" Someone's opposing view of YOU will only work "if" you're already opposing yourself within! Encouragement will never work "if" you've already "discouraged yourself within!" YOU perceive according to what YOU have "fed your Within!"

:: ::

Never allow someone else to become "your nerves!" That way "they can't ride what they don't own!" Be your own "keys!"

:: ::

Say to Yourself "My thoughts love Me!" "My WORDS believe in ME!" When Your Words trust YOU "their friends will too!"

:: ::

There is "no devil" in "my world!" And I see no reason to create one NOW! Anything that's "cast out" ain't coming back to visit!

:: ::

Love loses its Eternal life when we choose who receives it and who doesn't!

:: ::

I find it amazing that out of all of the "spiritual truths" that we may "know," our relationships and ideas of others, as well as our "own personal preferences of thought," are byproducts of the ideas of life that we're most comfortable with, even if those ideas and comforts differ from the Divine itself.

:: ::

In the midst of the everyday "quagmire" of life, decisions, obligations, bills, drama, lunch, "moods of all kinds and types," relationships, kids, phone calls, applications, acceptances and denials, are YOU yet maintaining a healthy recognition of Self and Identity? Just asking...

:: ::

A "spirituality" that constantly defines its relevance based on how many "temporal things" it can receive, is not "spirituality, but poverty!" Embrace true spirituality and "the temporal" will serve YOU, not define YOU!

:: ::

Limitations only exist when we declare them "alive!" Limitation is a result of an outlook that we create to reflect our own, self-imposed inability!

:: ::

True forgiveness "does not constantly remind that it's trying to forgive!"

:: ::

The "Unknown" is not always out "to get You!" Sometimes, "the Unknown" is seeking to Bless YOU! Stop conditioning Yourself "to always be afraid and anxious" when facing an "Unfamiliar Downpour of Positive Manifestations!"

:: ::

Never allow the "practical nuances" of your human condition "to weaken your confidence in Your Divine Nature!" Even Jesus "got hungry at times!"

:: ::

If YOU open your "eyes" and "see," You will find that You are in the midst of something AMAZING! The chaos around YOU, however, only confirms when your "eyes" are "closed!"

:: ::

The Powerful Thoughts of Love and Possibilities you daily entertain "will one day become the Angels that YOU may encounter without knowing!" You never know when Truths You live "will become a Person!"

:: ::

YOU "are not in poverty" because YOU still possess the ability to "have at least a Thought, and a Say, in your daily matters!" To be impoverished is to be void of Choice and not money! Unleash "the Wealth" of your Spirit and "serve it" with your Practice of Life!

:: ::

Live profoundly. Refrain from "reminding" others that you're not perfect. Refrain from "rebuilding" your Excuses. Refrain from sending out that invitation addressed to "unforeseen circumstances!"

:: ::

Your daily reality of logic, reasoning, perception, and perspective, reflects the Nature of whatever or whoever is God to YOU and in YOU! Your "daily Body of Work" reveals who, or what, our Spirit loves much of! Whatever it is I love "will make sure to give me all of it's strength and ability!"

:: ::

There is no need to "make sense" of everything Good that happens to Your life. Sometimes, "Sense" is the one thing that "ends all of the Momentum of Possibility!" Learn how to discern which things YOU should just simply "ALLOW!"

:: ::

We know how "limited" we've lived when Divine Acts of Goodness and Love towards us "are constantly feeling like a Surprise!" Live who YOU deserve to BE, so that what YOU deserve, WILL BE!

:: ::

Keep the Promise YOU made to Yourself! Distractions confirm that there is no confidence in the Significance of the Promise! But commitment to what You've promised Yourself confirms "that You've already determined the validity of your NOW and your Future!"

:: ::

Our Consciousness is as clear as the Forgiveness we've truly given, as well as the Love "we are loving with!" When my forgiveness is true "my uneasiness and discomforts with another cannot be maintained!" Your spirituality is not obligated to be complicated!

:: ::

Awesome thoughts, that are absent of one's natural action, are not beliefs, just "thoughts!" The "activities" of ones' natural action, through any issue of life's events, are "beliefs!" What we truly believe "are being naturally done every moment!"

:: ::

Frustration is when You're trying hard not to lose anything "before YOU even start!" Awaken that "hidden faith" within YOU!

:: ::

You've done your best "when the Future no longer sends YOU reminders to start over!" When it's finished to Him, it's finished with YOU!

:: ::

When YOU are a "peer" with your issues "instead of a Lord," your "commands" will be heard as an opinion instead of a Voice of Authority! NOW is the Time to recognize your Prophetic Sensitivity and Mastery!

:: ::

You are a living temple of The Divine. Speak to Yourself "and make it so" to Yourself!

:: ::

Nothing's "heavy" when YOU truly want "to pick it up!"

:: ::

The "Will of God" does not contain itself to an event, but is a "built-in Permission" that naturally serves as a Guide and Expanse to your daily realities of LIFE and MIND! If the Permission allows it "then SEIZE IT!"

:: ::

There is no devil in your "world" unless you're needing one! When YOU "create him," he will be there in the form of "fear, procrastination, and the need of excuse!" The "enemy disappears" when there is no need for these particular things!

:: ::

God isn't obligated to "build your LIFE" with the "tools, experiences, techniques, or even truths" that you're comfortable with! Comfortability is the reason that most of us "are yet stuck in the same place" while yet maintaining barren ideas. NOW is the TIME to PRACTICE something Bold and Original!

:: ::

The desire to "control" how much "control one is willing to lose" is the very thing that keeps us "controlled by fear, doubt, and the inability to fully experience a valid, long lasting, personal discovery!" Our fear of "being pulled away too far" is the very thing that keeps us living in shallow waters and immature life realities!

:: ::

Deep Thought is not found relevant in it's inability to grasp or understand, but in it's power to make access to the past realities of limitation, fear, and doubt "an impossible place to revisit or re-conceive!"

:: ::

Unless YOU determine if YOU are right "for" YOU, you won't know who or what is right "with" YOU!" Are YOU right "for YOU?"

:: ::

Don't just "say" that YOU deserve something Good! KNOW WHY You deserve it! Don't be afraid to "evaluate the Intentions of your Heart, Mind, and Soul!" You're too great to not know the "fullness of your own INNER HOUSE!"

:: ::

Is the pain of "losing Yourself" greater than the pain of being "rejected" by someone else? Your level of "pain" and "come back" is determined by "Who" or "What" YOU desire to be defined and validated by Most!

:: ::

If You're afraid of the Truth of YOU "then the lies about YOU will win!"

:: ::

There is nothing against YOU. The only "war" You're facing are the "hidden, comfortable perspectives" that are telling YOU that life would be much easier "if YOU would release Yourself from the inconveniences of Discipline, Sureness and Originality!" Power recognized is a Power maintained!

:: ::

Is it easier to give "love that no one can see" to a Person "that cannot be seen" than to give what YOU can plainly see and feel "to someone YOU must see all the time?" When we love WHO WE SEE amongst us, our unseen Love to an Unseen God "becomes a Manifested Experience!"

:: ::

Continue "forgiving" Yourselves from the very darkness that fuels the constant cycles of "life-imbalance" you may experience in life. Forgiveness is not in the "constant apologizing" to Yourself but in granting Yourself permission to evolve, mature, and expand, without fear of "repeating the same mistakes and disappointments again!" Allowing the Power of LETTING IT BE WHAT IT BE!

:: ::

An "altar" cannot put God in YOU. He is already within YOU! But it's up to YOU, however, to determine how much of HIM you want to Realize! Little God, "little sight!" Great God "great sight!" Unlimited God, "unlimited sight!" YOU are the "altar" that determines the reality of who God truly is to YOU. So, how much are YOU willing for your life to "SEE?"

:: ::

Decisions that remove YOU from a certain dimension of tolerant enslavement, comfort zones of the mediocre, or self imposed limitations that exempt YOU from the accountability of Mastery, can cause pain and feelings of unsureness at times! Decisions only cause Pain when Your "weakness" is leaving Your Body!

:: ::

People who despise the constant positiveness in another "will never have any!" They will assure themselves of a consistently unbalanced world of ups and downs and will be obligated to find tolerance of that misery by calling it "LIFE!"

:: ::

Never become so addicted to hearing your own sounds of "unpracticed thoughts of wisdom" that YOU fear the actual experience of DOING the Wisdom itself! The greatest procrastinators are some of life's "smartest people!" Be, live, and DO, "your thoughts of Power!"

:: ::

Your daily "manifestations" are byproducts of your "subconscious meditations!" What YOU "say" is not done by "mouth" but by "soul!" Your "inner Self" creates everything YOU experience! Your mouth "merely houses teeth!"

:: ::

Live Profound with no excuse. No one is obligating You to remind yourself that the conditions around You are imperfect.

Live with Joy "just because!" Reminding yourself of misery "will only allow the misery to remain!" Conditions should never be given the power to determine Your Path and Power!

:: ::

The worst thing YOU can do is to allow Misery to "paralyze" YOU by wallowing in its "arms of Do-Nothingness!" Make a Decision and GET UP! The "comfort YOU feel in wallowing" is not "Thinking" or "ME-TIME," but life slowly being drained from within and death becoming a close friend! GET UP!

:: ::

To love, and not Tell, is just as dangerous as to Tell and not love! Everyone is left with NOTHING! So, do more than "tell someone that YOU love them!" LOVE THEM...

:: ::

Are YOU giving yourself permission, as well as the allowance, to feel "good" today? We're accustomed to living "empty" while "allowing others to deposit various states of BEING and FEELING within US!" NOW, you possess the capacity to "make Your own BETTERMENT deposits within YOU!" It's not like YOU "didn't have the power in the first place!"

:: ::

I have found that anything I truly desired to do "I did, without fear!" And Anything I "had to do without desire," was performed with anxiety, fear, and incompetence! Are YOU living what YOU desire, or what You HAVE TO?

WHAT RESONATED WITH YOU
ABOUT THIS CHAPTER?

_____

_____

_____

_____

_____

_____

_____

_____

_____

_____

_____

_____

_____

_____

_____

_____

_____

_____

WHAT WAS YOUR "KEY WORD OR THOUGHT" FROM THIS CHAPTER?

_____

_____

_____

_____

_____

_____

_____

_____

_____

_____

_____

_____

_____

_____

_____

_____

_____

_____

WHAT ARE YOU GOING TO DO NOW?

_____

_____

_____

_____

_____

_____

_____

_____

_____

_____

_____

_____

_____

_____

_____

_____

_____

_____

_____

_____

WHEN WILL YOU GET STARTED?

WHY HAVEN'T YOU STARTED?

Affirmation Part V
THE POWER OF ORIGINAL THOUGHT

INTRODUCTION

It is a very bold move to live Original in a world "full of copies!" Really, your Originality should be as natural as breathing! No effort needed. No force intended! Original Life is where your power resides. Naturally divine. Naturally free. Naturally creative.

The Mindset from this LIFE naturally sets itself apart from the comforts of familiar acceptance and "impoverished human existence!" I do not mean "impoverished" by the lack of financial gain, but by ones lack of discovering their Purpose of existence! When you have not determined "why you were born," you have not determined "if" you are alive! And if you are not "alive," it is impossible for you to be "heard!"

When YOU have not only "found yourself," but have "accepted" who YOU have found to be YOU, a boldness to live and be set apart will overwhelm YOU "and empower YOU to exist in a way YOU have never existed before!"

And the Thoughts begin NOW!!

Your Authenticity of Self is as Powerful and Profound "as the excuses YOU can live without, as well as the procrastinations You are no longer in need of!"

:: ::

BE, "no matter how the Atmosphere is acting!"

:: ::

Impossible to know Jesus and feel unworthy at the same time. When you awaken to The life, "WORTH of SELF" is the first gift You experience! Love Him as YOU LOVE YOU!

:: ::

In my dreams "I never die!" Maybe if we live our dreams we can "break the appointment" and awaken the Eternity that lives within all of US!

:: ::

Whatever YOU "can feel" also has "an ear" to listen to your Voice! What are YOU "instructing it to do?"

:: ::

As a result of refraining myself from "trying to set straight the many opinions that were formed against me," I restored years to my lifetime, incredible perspectives to my Mind, and strength to my body! Accept the fact that Your life is too big "to be viewed as one thing!"

:: ::

When a Positive Force is thinking of YOU "sudden shifts will awaken around YOU, even without your prior knowledge of it!" Thoughts of Goodness that have YOU in Mind "will provide the daily momentums of Your Day!" Now, Think lovely towards someone else!

:: ::

Spiritual Poverty is the result of actually thinking that God is threatened by US standing "on our own two feet, creating from our Imagination, and establishing Influence in the world!" God is more excited than ever when we realize "our Divine Reality!" He is saddened when we obligate ourselves "to live without BEING!"

:: ::

The BEST THINGS in life are results of making the Best Decision in the midst of an Incredibly Divine Opportunity! YOU BECOME "what You do with God when faced with GOD!"

:: ::

Out of all of the "cool truths" we consistently hear, I find that Your best Life is created from Decisions that You've overcome the fear to make! Life doesn't establish its goodness from hearing only, but in the "doing" after the hearing!

:: ::

Everyday, YOU experience the things that dominate "your

attention!" Whatever, or Whoever it is that "owns your attention," will "tend" to YOU, your Mind, and your Spirit! It is within YOU to create either "Power or Pitifulness!"

:: ::

Whatever your true calling is "will be felt within YOU," and not given to YOU from someone else's opinion! A "calling" is that One Thing that constantly "invites" YOU to the Reason YOU were Born and the Reasons YOU must remain ALIVE! Listen to Your Heart "if you're bold enough!"

:: ::

The love and authenticity of Self that YOU feel, after someone has blessed YOU with their mere presence, is the "Gospel of LIFE!" It is imperative for YOU to feel your "most realest" after Truth has graced your presence! If you feel otherwise "You have not yet met the Truth!"

:: ::

Judge not my words or the way I say them, "but judge me according to the feelings of Possibility, Love, and Power that You feel within Yourself after experiencing my presence!" Judge me righteously! For the love you feel within YOU confirms the Truth of everything I will ever BE about!

:: ::

Whatever it is YOU believe "will cause the best and worst things" to be said about YOU! YOU cannot receive the

Best of that Belief "unless YOU are willing to endure the worst that others think or say about YOU" because of that belief! YOU BECOME what you have believed!

:: ::

Perfection, without purpose, is "imperfect." YOU, however, "are perfect enough." YOU deserve to "enter the Room!"

:: ::

Never let the fear of others "getting the wrong idea" keep You from living Your most truest Self, as well as loving from your most Significant Love! Never allow Yourself to "live un-original" for the sake of what someone "might perceive!" A limited mind will create whatever idea they want to entertain the most of.

:: ::

The Significance of Your life is not determined by how many of your prayers are answered but by the profound capacity to "remain steadfast to your BEING" in any Season, through any Shift, and through many seemingly unexplainable circumstances YOU may experience while evolving! Sons "don't beg!" We just BE...

:: ::

REALITY is whatever "is real" to YOU! It is YOU who decides if you are rich or poor, successful or "in the process of!" Never let "a picture" decide for You. You would be surprised at how many of us are "chasing after a standard" that was created by the opinion of another. Your HEART will let YOU know "when Significance has arrived FOR YOU!"

:: ::

Whatever our perspective of Spirituality may be, let it be one that "empowers the most hopeless soul to Love again, Dream again, Imagine again, and to live Life torment free!" If I am not allowed to "see" by your spirituality, then I am but another "pawn" in the hands of those who seek to control my soul with the "fear of BEING!"

:: ::

Failure should be viewed as a "circumstance" that painstakingly takes so long to realize that one would give up their search to obtain it!

:: ::

Living anything "less than Original" will always have you in constant torment as you seek approval and acceptance! Only when YOU exist "as the Real YOU" will you experience Peace and a "natural essence of Empowerment" that cannot be "understood" by anything, or anyone who lives "less than Original!"

:: ::

Become a "daily, living Wisdom!" For ignorance destroys all things, "even when it's quiet." Not knowing what YOU should know "will keep what should be KNOWN from being known!" Allow yourself to become "living Wisdom, living Knowledge, and living Power!"

:: ::

Be the essence of God to everything "and YOU will no longer be the victim of crazy situations" but the creator of Moments "that are Divine!"

:: ::

Love is loving YOU as we speak. It is the most Perfect Love you will ever experience in your lifetime. There is never a moment "where YOU are unloved!"

:: ::

YOU constantly have in your life "the things that trust You most!" You possess the Power to change "what's trusting" You as well!

:: ::

Give others the Love "that's loving YOU!" Grant them the mercy "that's forgiving YOU!" Give them the freedom of doubt "that You want others to give YOU!" You can only create from the Truth you practice "and not the Truths you fear!"

:: ::

You may confirm the Teachings you've had, "but the reactions from the Atmosphere will confirm the lessons You've learned from them!"

:: ::

When Guilt and Torment loses its Power, the capacity to live, Imagine, and BE expands without limit! The "prince of guilt" can find nothing in YOU "when YOU live as The King!"

:: ::

I must see, feel, and sense the relevance of myself in this world "in order for my Words to do the same!" WE ARE our Words. When we feel "disconnected within our souls", our words are mere "letters!" But when we are ONE, our Words become MANIFESTATIONS of a divine mind!

:: ::

The "highest Love" will naturally love "without determining WHO!" It has an amazing ability to "love EVERYWHERE and ANYHOW!" Difference, of any kind, cannot affect it. It only expands it...

:: ::

BECOME the Person "that will connect YOU to the greatest life-Changing Opportunity of your LIFE!"

:: ::

God never sent us to here to "believe," but to BE! Everything else is appointed to follow...

:: ::

In order for me to become a great Man, I must first become

"a Great Wife" of the Divine!

:: ::

Church is not the only Place YOU should hear God. Your Mind, at times, "can be the Teacher that leads YOU to Incredible Heights, or the enemy that destroys your ability to dream!" It is from within "that your Vision or Blindness is determined!"

:: ::

ONENESS of life "is a beautiful, passionate partnership between Humanity and Divinity!" Feed them equally for maximum performance!

:: ::

Your "words" have no desire to be more powerful "than Your actions!" Your dreams have no desire to simply reside in your Mind! And your Identity is not complete if it cannot withstand the misjudgment of others! Live Profound in every moment!

:: ::

Become the "Somebody" that loves YOU with all their heart! Gift your existence with Wholeness, Power, Intelligence, and Supernatural living! Leaving YOU is impossible for God to do!

:: ::

What are YOU doing to "affirm" that You SHOULD NOT believe in Yourself? If You find nothing there, proceed to live empowered, necessary, and significant! If You HAVE FOUND something, "let's eradicate it with the essence of our Divinity… together!"

:: ::

A "Life Solution" that arrives unexpectedly has a way of "awakening the hidden excuse in YOU" if You're not careful. The Visionary must always condition themselves to expect an encounter with NOW!

:: ::

If you have to "get in character and mind" in order to "do" your beliefs, then what you believe "is not really your beliefs!" Whatever YOU truly have conformed to "has already developed and determined your natural character of life and mind!" Simply continue in the Evolution of Yourself!

:: ::

As powerful as NOW is, it still must submit itself to a decision! Just because you lack now doesn't mean your future is poverty! And if you're "mighty" now doesn't mean you will conquer the world tomorrow! NOW can, and cannot, tell the future at the same time. It must submit itself to the greatness of a decision you commit to!

:: ::

What others choose to ignore about You "doesn't change how blessed you really are!" Live on in The Light, even when the "eyes of others are closed!"

:: ::

Religion makes you better, but Discovery will make you YOURSELF!

:: ::

Quiet your soul. Listen. Learn. We're not always able to determine who'll be gracious enough to "overlook our ignorance and wink at it!" No one else is responsible to "protect our emotions" when it comes to validating our existence, significance, and worth!

:: ::

Take every "aha" moment to new dimensions of action! I have found that "undone ideas" torment my life the most! It makes no sense for a beautiful world to remain hidden "within the fears of the soul!"

:: ::

You must awaken the courage that allows life and everything within it "to conform" to what You have spoken! Embrace this Boldness, not just to "speak a thing," but to allow what was said "to change everything you know!"

:: ::

To some, a "dream come true" is obtaining the desired result "without change, effort, or discipline!" Not so, not so! Most have missed their Divine Appointment simply because "change and a shift in habit" was involved! Don't let this be YOU!

:: ::

YOU are the deciding factor between what is possible and what is not! Your energy will "totally agree" with whatever you decide!

:: ::

Don't "cosign" for other people's "wars!" Their "depression" will seek you out, even though you're not responsible for their issues! Don't live blind!

:: ::

Never give mistakes the advantage over You! We've all made them. Rise up. Your boldness in living and loving confirms your forgiveness of self!

:: ::

Stop "watering down" and apologizing for your uniqueness! There's nothing wrong with your style! Those who can't appreciate it "will always ask you to change!"

:: ::

When journeying to the next Chapter of your life, the first thing that needs to be "removed" in order to maximize the experience, is not another person, but your own "thoughts, perceptions, and fears" that contaminated the reality You were living in before! When WE SHIFT "everything else will follow!"

:: ::

YOU become known by the "enemies" you defeat, as well as the issues you've conquered that "appear larger than life!" It's within YOU, as YOU, to do it!

:: ::

When You're truly ready "you'll make UP your mind!" Even God doesn't believe in transformation without conviction...

:: ::

If you never rise up to get what's yours "you never wanted it, or its not yours!" Don't get angry if someone else obtains it!

:: ::

When You KNOW Yourself FULLY "You won't mind being questioned!" When You're "The Answer", questions become your servants!

:: ::

Possibilities, or Impossibilities, are simply matters of "choice and thought!" You will "name a Thing" based on "the Ability You want to experience Most!" Really and truly, YOU have Dominion over everything!

:: ::

You will naturally "live" what YOU feel YOU have "permission" to live! When "Permission" is known the need for confirmation of a thing will become a relic of the past!

:: ::

When problems despise YOU, they become your "issues!" When problems respect YOU, however, they become your Solutions! Live your Godness and stop apologizing for it!

:: ::

LIFE "is what You feed it!" And it will naturally "pull YOU" in the direction of the "taste" it craves most!

:: ::

Grant others the privilege of misjudging YOU, but to misjudge Yourself is unacceptable!"

:: ::

The Fight was won long before You were born. Everything you may be facing now "is merely personal!" All you have to do now "is Command!"

:: ::

Feelings cannot be taught "how to feel". They are the "inner geniuses" that remind YOU that YOU do have a choice. And when Self is mastered, feelings will follow your Lead!

:: ::

Accept Yourself unconditionally! Don't just "speak and see Yourself as Great, but accept it as a fully legitimate reality!" Your Mind will " never allow Your body to do" what YOU don't think it has a right to do! Comfort is the "father of excuse!"

::   ::

Live from an Identity that causes "Great Things to constantly ask for YOU!" See if Greatness has enough credit worthiness "to obtain the residence of someone, like YOU!" If the elements can pay the taxes of Jesus, "surely it will seek to do the same for YOU!"

::   ::

One true Friend is greater than a thousand associates!

::   ::

Begin to send Thoughts of Goodness, Strategies, and Wholeness to one another Right NOW as we speak! Begin to desire for others to experience Peace, Responsibility, and Purpose. While you're doing that, "allow your lives to become instruments of Impartation and a Conduit for every Significant Moment of Power when it arises!"

WHAT RESONATED WITH YOU
ABOUT THIS CHAPTER?

_____

_____

_____

_____

_____

_____

_____

_____

_____

_____

_____

_____

_____

_____

_____

_____

_____

_____

_____

_____

What Was Your "KEY WORD or THOUGHT" from this Chapter?

_____

_____

_____

_____

_____

_____

_____

_____

_____

_____

_____

_____

_____

_____

_____

_____

_____

WHAT ARE YOU GOING TO DO NOW?

_____

_____

_____

_____

_____

_____

_____

_____

_____

_____

_____

_____

_____

_____

_____

_____

_____

_____

_____

WHEN WILL YOU GET STARTED?

WHY HAVEN'T YOU STARTED?

_____

_____

_____

_____

_____

_____

_____

_____

_____

_____

_____

_____

_____

_____

_____

_____

_____

_____

_____

_____

ABOUT THE AUTHOR

Undrai Fizer enjoys life as an author, teacher, and accomplished jazz pianist, creating the original genre of "consciousness" music.

Not only is he a practitioner of divine principle and life, he is also the founder and CEO of Kairos Inter-Global, a module formulated to provoke and inspire thoughts that lead to personal and spiritual enlightenment, purpose, and awakening. He shares his life with Bridget E. Fizer and their three sons Benjamin, Loren, and Zion in the city of Houston, Texas.